THE CHRISTIAN CHURCH'S LGBTQ FAILURE

MOVE TOWARD A BIBLICAL APPROACH OF SPEAKING THE TRUTH IN LOVE

PETER DEHAAN

Library of Congress Control Number: 2023921971

Published by Rock Rooster Books, Grand Rapids, Michigan

ISBNs:

- 979-8-88809-064-0 (e-book)
- 979-8-88809-065-7 (paperback)
- 979-8-88809-066-4 (hardcover)
- 979-8-88809-067-1 (audiobook)

Credits:

- Developmental editor: Julie Harbison
- Copy editor: Robyn Mulder
- Cover design: Cassidy Wierks
- Author photo: Chelsie Jensen Photography

~

The personal accounts in this book are all based on real people and their stories. All names have been changed. Most descriptions are composites of multiple individuals. Therefore, any resemblance to an actual person is coincidental. Read these narratives as creative nonfiction.

To Everyone Who Struggles and Those Who Care
About Them

CONTENTS

HOW IT ALL BEGAN

In this book I'll make no effort to be politically correct. I will, however, strive to be biblically correct. This distinction is critical.

If this goal upsets you, don't bother to continue reading as it will thoroughly offend you. And if you're not open to having your perspective challenged, this book will only cause you angst.

But if you're willing to consider a different approach to this most contentious of subjects, then proceed with expectation. As you read, pray for the Holy Spirit to speak to you and inform your thinking.

The Holy Spirit, in fact, is why I wrote this book. It wasn't my idea, and I didn't want to do it, but I am obeying the direction given to me by the Holy Spirit.

Though the underpinnings of this book may have been brewing for years, the catalyst came to me supernaturally after watching the movie *Jesus Revolution*.

Jesus Revolution is based on events in the late 60s and early 70s, when a pastor in Southern California welcomes hippies to his church—despite some initial personal reluctance—when all other churches rejected them. What happened then touches me profoundly now.

Jesus Revolution is based on real-world events. Though taking place over fifty years ago, the example is still relevant today, reminding us of the power of Jesus and his life-changing message. It clawed at status quo Christianity, in favor of a fresh faith expression that reached those on the outside. In this case, it was hippies.

It's easy to say that, had I been an adult at that time, I'd have embraced hippies in my faith community. Yet, in truth, I suspect I'd have also pulled away like most everyone else. I fear I'd have lacked the vision—and the courage—to embrace a countercultural group of people.

"How does this apply now?" I asked myself.

"Who are today's hippies that most churches dismiss?"

I squirmed a bit when I realized it's those who identify as LGBTQ.

At the same time, the Holy Spirit urged me to write a book about it.

Frankly, I didn't want to. I feared I'd upset everyone, and I prefer to avoid the drama. I may lack courage.

Yet if God calls me to do it, I'll do it.

Let's begin.

A FIRM FOUNDATION

As Jesus wraps up his longest recorded message, the Sermon on the Mount, he talks about two hypothetical people: a wise man and a foolish man.

The Teacher says that anyone who hears his words *and* obeys them is like a wise man who builds his house on a rock-stable foundation. When rain pours, floodwaters rise, and wind buffets the house, it will stand firm because it's on a rock-solid foundation. So, too, are we when we base our faith on Jesus's words and obey them.

But those who hear Jesus's words and don't obey are like a foolish man who builds his house on sandy ground. When rain pours, floodwaters rise, and wind buffets the house, the ground washes away and the house crumbles. So, too, are those who ignore Jesus's words and don't obey them (Matthew 7:24–27).

Therefore, we need to build a firm faith foundation. And this foundation is on Jesus's words and our obedience to them. We find Jesus's words in the Bible. They're primarily in Matthew, Mark, Luke, and John (along with Acts, 1 Corinthians, 2 Corinthians, and Revelation).

Yet we must realize that Jesus and the Father are one. They, along with the Holy Spirit, are God—the God revealed in the Bible. God's words—from the Father, Son, and Holy Spirit—occur throughout Scripture. What one says, they all say. And we must heed what they tell us to do.

The Bible contains the words of God. As such, it becomes our faith foundation. It is *the* Word of God. As Jesus said, anyone who hears his words—that is, the words of God—and obeys them is a wise person who establishes their faith on the firm foundation of Scripture.

Yes, God's words, as found in the Bible, are the foundation of our faith.

Anchored or Untethered?

If we don't anchor our beliefs in a scriptural foundation, our faith becomes untethered. It has no footing. That's why we need an unshakable basis for the truth about God. Without a solid foundation, we will inevitably disconnect what Jesus said about how we should believe and act from what we actually think and do.

Because of this, we must cling to the words of the Bible as the foundation for our faith. If we veer from biblical truth, we end up making God into whoever we want him to be. We forget we were created in God's image (Genesis 1:26–28).

Instead, many try to make God into *their* image. This is folly.

These misguided people take the parts of the Bible they like and dismiss the rest. It's as though they read it with a highlighter in one hand and a pair of scissors in the other. In doing so they forget what Paul says. He writes that all Scripture comes from God and is useful to us (2 Timothy 3:16).

That's *all* Scripture.

Not only the parts they like but also the parts they disagree with or don't understand, and especially those passages that make them squirm.

Paul further warns that a time will come when people won't accept sound doctrine. They'll tweak God's truth to conform to their own ideas. And they'll surround themselves with teachers who will tell them what they long to hear instead of what Scripture has long proclaimed. They'll exchange the truth for lies (2 Timothy 4:3–4).

Biblically Correct or Politically Correct?

In doing so, they replace the parts of Scripture they don't like with the world's perspective. This makes them feel good about themselves. They become politically correct, with society's mutable views replacing God's unchangeable truth.

They do as they see fit and not what God says. But this is not a recent problem. See Judges 17:6 and Judges 21:25. It's an old issue that's reemerged under the guise of secular enlightenment. But at its core, it is sinful people rebelling against God.

When they try to create their own belief system, they deviate from the truth—the reality of who God is. They build their spiritual existence and eternal hope on a foundation of sand. It will not last. Though they may feel good about the religion they've created, it provides them with nothing of value for this world or the next. It will not sustain them and means nothing.

The result is a gospel of human origin, which Paul opposes (Galatians 1:11). Instead, they need the full gospel of Jesus and not just part of it mixed with what they decide to add to it.

A religion they make up can't save them.

Godly Worship or Idol Worship?

This manufacturing of their own theology is idol worship, the idol of self. The Old Testament prophets warn against bowing down to idols, of worshiping manmade gods.

Habakkuk asks, "What value does an idol have that a craftsman creates?" The one who makes it trusts in his own creation (Habakkuk 2:18).

Similarly, Jeremiah likens idols that cannot speak to a scarecrow that's placed in a field. It must be carried because it cannot walk. "Don't fear them," he warns. "They can do no harm nor any good" (Jeremiah 10:5).

In his prophecy, Isaiah has a long rant about the foolishness of worshiping idols. These are forged from metal, chiseled out of rock, or carved from wood. A man cuts down a tree. He uses part of the log for firewood, and he fashions the other part into an idol. He prays to it, but it is not alive. It cannot hear the petition or answer the request. For such a person, this is like trying to find sustenance by eating ashes. His heart misleads him. He can't save himself (Isaiah 44:9–20).

Though we don't make physical idols anymore, many people make intellectual ones. These cerebral idols are more deadly because they're not tangible. These idols hide in the minds of their creators. People who think this way enjoy a smug confidence in the theology that their intellect has fashioned, yet they have veered too far from the truth of God's words. They have constructed a religion that lacks the firm foundation of biblical truth. When the rain comes, their house of false faith will wash away. When the wind blows, it will collapse.

Through their intellect, they choose to reject some of the truth that God says and replace it with a fabricated theology that makes them feel good about themselves, their priorities, and their life choices. This perspective shows that they question the Word of God.

God's Truth or Human Deception

With the Bible as the foundation of our faith, the truth it contains is absolute. The idea of asserting anything as absolute truth in today's culture is politically incorrect. Yet I don't care what the prevailing winds of our culture think about truth. Many people say that it's something we can make up, doing whatever seems right to us.

They are wrong, and the Bible is right.

God does not change and neither does his Word (James 1:17). He doesn't change his mind (Numbers 23:19). Therefore, God's Word is absolute. We can't make truth to be whatever we want it to be and expect it to accomplish anything worthwhile.

Jesus proclaims himself as truth. He says he is the way, the truth, and the life. The only way we can truly know Father God is to come to him through Jesus as the truth (John 14:6).

John writes that we will know the truth and the truth will set us free (John 8:32). This truth is Jesus and his teaching. Those who reject the truth cannot be saved (2 Thessalonians 2:10). I repeat, those who reject the truth cannot be saved.

It is our knowledge of this truth that leads to godliness (Titus 1:1). Whereas the truth that others make up cannot accomplish this. Instead, it leads to the opposite. It leads to ungodliness, which results in death.

Yet we must be careful how we proclaim biblical truth. It isn't a weapon to use to attack others. Instead, we are to speak the truth in love (Ephesians 4:15). In love, we may need to whisper the truth instead of shouting it. Sometimes, we may even need to be quiet and let our actions speak for us.

Believe God or Question God?

The reaction of these people who question God's truth is nothing new.

Let's go back to Adam and Eve in the garden of Eden. It's not long before they question God's word. This starts when the crafty serpent misleads Eve. (John later confirms that the serpent is the devil, also known as Satan, in Revelation 12:9 and 20:2).

The sly serpent eases up to Eve. "Did God really say you can't eat from any tree in the garden?" (Genesis 3:1). He's trying to plant doubt in her mind.

But she corrects him; he misquoted God. "It's not all trees," she says, "just one" (Genesis 2:16–17 and 3:2–3).

When the serpent realizes he can't fool her by misrepresenting what God said, he gets more blatant. He says that God lied. We know that God doesn't lie (Numbers 23:19), but Eve doesn't know this.

The serpent is persuasive. Eve chooses to reject what God said and believe the serpent instead. She takes the fruit from the forbidden tree and eats it. She gives some to Adam, and he eats it too. As a result of their disobedience, God expels them from their idyllic garden paradise and punishes all three (Genesis 3:14–19).

The psalmist later writes that he has hidden God's word in his heart so that he won't sin against his creator (Psalm 119:11). We'll do well to follow this example. Though Eve correctly remembered what God said, she hadn't internalized it enough to keep her from sinning.

Know Scripture or Be Misled?

Let's fast forward to the New Testament and the life of Jesus. The Holy Spirit prompts Jesus to go to the wilderness, where Jesus fasts for forty days (Matthew 4:1–11). His body is drained. It's now, when Jesus is at his weakest, that the devil tempts the Savior to abort his mission.

Satan encourages Jesus to turn stones into bread so he'll have something to eat. Performing a miracle will also confirm his power.

But Jesus doesn't fall for the enemy's trap. Instead, Jesus quotes Scripture, saying that we don't live by bread alone but on the words of our Lord God (Deuteronomy 8:3).

Next, Satan takes Jesus to a lofty vantage. From there they survey all the nations throughout the world. Satan, who for a time controls it, promises to give it to Jesus if he will merely bow down to worship him.

Jesus won't, and again quotes Scripture. It says we are to worship and serve only the Lord God (Deuteronomy 6:13).

Having twice failed, the devil now likewise quotes Scripture. From the highest point of the temple, Satan taunts Jesus. "*If* you are the Son of God, jump. Scripture says God will send his angels to protect you and keep you from harm" (Psalm 91:11–12).

The devil questions Jesus's divinity as God's Son, which begs for Jesus to defend his identity. But he doesn't. Instead, he responds with a Scripture verse of his own. He says to not test the Lord God (Deuteronomy 6:16).

Jesus knows Scripture. He has hidden it in his heart. It is his foundation.

May we do likewise. May we not deviate from it, regardless of what the world says.

MY FRIEND DAVID

My wife and I were part of an urban church that attracted people from the fringe of society—a lot of them. As a group, we specialized in welcoming everyone, accepting them without judgment. They needed a safe place where they could experience Jesus, and our church gave it to them. My wife and I embraced this vision.

When David showed up, I treated him like everyone else there. I accepted him as a person and listened to what he had to say. David began attending more regularly and would often look for me after the service.

I don't remember when or how he told me he was gay, but I learned this early on. He never talked about a boyfriend or dating, but he often talked about a gay support group he was involved with and hoped to lead next semester. He talked little about his faith, but it was obvious he had some church experience in his background.

Week by week he shared more about his story. He attended the local community college and didn't have a car. He relied on public transportation to get to school and home each day. But the buses didn't run on Sunday, so he walked to church. It took him an hour and a half. When I learned this, I offered him a ride home, even though it was in the opposite direction from ours.

He gladly accepted. His apartment building—a large house subdivided into multiple units—was easy enough to find. He insisted we drop him off at the curb in front, even though his entrance was in the back. On the Sundays we saw him after church, we'd offer to drive him home. On most Sundays, he was glad to accept.

After several weeks, he asked us to drop him off at the local grocery store instead. He was out of food and needed to pick up a few things. He said he could walk home. It would take him fifteen minutes.

This is when we learned he went to the grocery store every few days. He did this because he could only buy what he could carry. We told him to buy everything he needed, and we'd drive him home.

My wife and I waited in the car while he shopped. It took him forever, but eventually he pushed out a shopping cart with seven bags of groceries. We drove him home, but he insisted we wait in the car while he unloaded.

After that, taking him to the store after church became a common occurrence. My wife would keep him company as he shopped to nudge him away from distractions and help him make his selections. I wisely waited in the car, as my goal in shopping is to get in and get out as fast as possible. My presence would not be good for any of us.

When the semester ended, he said he would be gone for a while. We didn't see him for several months. And when we did, he kept us at a distance and declined our offer of a ride home. We never saw him again after that day.

Although I had allowed him to control our conversations and only reacted to what he said, I wonder if I should have been more intentional and guided our discussion to spiritual matters. I wonder what I should have done differently. And I wonder how he is and what he's doing today. I pray that Jesus is part of his life.

LESSONS FROM THE
GOOD SAMARITAN

Doctor Luke writes about a religious expert who comes to Jesus with a question.

"What must I do to inherit eternal life?" the man asks the Teacher.

Jesus turns the question back at him. "What does the law say?"

The man has a ready answer, which he gives in two parts, quoting from Deuteronomy 6:5 and Leviticus 19:18. "First is to love God completely," he says. "And second is to love your neighbor as much as you love yourself."

Jesus commends the man's wise answer and tells him to do just that.

Perhaps recalling the popular saying to "love

your neighbor and hate your enemy" (Matthew 5:43), the man asks Jesus for clarity. "Who is my neighbor?" He wants to know who he must love and who he can hate.

By way of an answer, Jesus gives the man a parable. We often call it the parable of the good Samaritan. Here's how it goes:

A man travels between two cities. He walks alone. Robbers attack him. They take his clothes, beat him, and leave him to die.

A priest comes along. He sees the dying man but doesn't want to get involved. He walks around him. Next, a Levite comes along and has the same reaction. Both avoid helping the hurting man. Though it doesn't make it right, both men could be adhering to the Law, especially if they might come in contact with a dead body, which would make them unclean.

After the two Jewish men ignore the injured man lying on the road, a Samaritan comes along.

Let's pause our story for a moment.

A Samaritan is a person the Jewish people look down on. Good Jews view Samaritans as less-than and avoid all interaction. They perceive it as a righteous act, a religious response. So when Jesus's Jewish audience hears him mention a Samaritan, they certainly gasp at the dramatic turn his parable is taking.

Now we resume the story.

The Samaritan takes pity on this suffering man and wants to help. He goes to him, treats his wounds, and carries him to town on his own donkey —while he walks. He gets a room in the local inn and tends to the man. The next day he pays the innkeeper for the room and instructs him to watch over the man as he recovers. The Samaritan pledges to pay the innkeeper for any additional expenses.

This story certainly repels the religious expert, along with Jesus's Jewish audience, because the Samaritan is the hero, while the Jewish priest and Levite are not.

Jesus concludes by asking the religious expert, "Which of the three was a neighbor to the injured man?"

The religious expert can't bring himself to speak the word *Samaritan*. Instead, he merely answers "the one who offered mercy."

Jesus tells him to do the same to others.

Through this parable, we see that the neighbor we're supposed to love is anyone who needs help. Our neighbor, therefore, is everyone who needs mercy and compassion. By implication, there is no one we can hate—at least not from God's perspective.

We should do likewise, loving our neighbors.

But there's even more to this passage. Recall the opening premise. The religious leader asks Jesus what he must do to inherit eternal life. His question is about salvation.

Jesus's answer isn't just about what we believe. It's also about who we love. Through this parable Jesus teaches us that we inherit eternal life when we love our neighbor. And our neighbor is anyone who needs our help. This includes people who identify as LGBTQ.

May we rightly love them in Jesus's name. It's a salvation issue. Jesus says so. And so does James when he says that believing means nothing if it doesn't produce action (James 2:26).

ALEXIS'S STORY

Alexis dated boys in high school. A lot of them. But they made demands while she wanted to wait. And the boys from church were worse. She hoped college would be different.

Here's her story:

The guys in college were even more of a challenge to deal with than the guys in high school. I went on a lot of first dates but few second ones. I wouldn't give them what they wanted.

The girls in my dorm had their own issues. There was this kind of unspoken sorority that they formed in response to how the guys treated them. Their attitudes were both petty and manipulative—and not at all chaste.

But I found a group of girls who were different. I started hanging out with them. We connected.

Imagine my surprise when I learned they were all lesbians. But I felt comfortable around them—and safe. Before I knew it, I was dating one of them. At first, this made me uncomfortable, but I reminded myself that she treated me better than most of the guys I had gone out with. In time I became okay with public displays of affection and would allow her to hold my hand in public.

I went home on the weekends whenever I could. One Sunday after church, I got brave and told my parents about my girlfriend. They were none too happy to hear about this. After some yelling and much crying, hugs eventually followed.

I told them there was nothing in the Bible that said two girls couldn't get married. They accepted my statement, but I hoped they would counter it. I wanted to know what Scripture said about this. I also pledged I'd find the right girl, and we'd make a lifelong commitment to each other.

After that I didn't feel comfortable going to church. Though my parents insisted they hadn't told anyone, I felt everyone at church looked at me differently. Or maybe it was my issue. Soon I stopped going. It was easier that way.

I miss not being part of a faith community and having people to encourage me on my spiritual journey, but I shoved that aside. I've found a new community of people who embrace me and love me for who I am.

Though my lesbian friends never talk about God or spiritual matters, it's a tradeoff I'm willing to make for their acceptance.

Alexis never did find a girl to settle down with and marry. Instead, she's had a series of relationships and embraced a morality of serial monogamy. She claims she's still a Christian, but she's not part of a church community and doesn't have a faith family.

Her lesbian friends are her family. They're all she has because of the strained relationship with her parents. She knows they still love her, but she's uncomfortable around them.

TYPES OF CHURCHES

We'll start our discussion of churches by looking at some general types of congregations. In doing so we'll avoid applying common labels to them. Labels are a convenient tool to categorize and generalize what something represents. Yet labels can confuse as much as clarify. This is especially true when they are emotion laden.

In their place, we'll apply new labels that don't carry preconceived notions or historical baggage. We'll call these three forms of congregations the type A church, the type B church, and the type C church.

To be clear, each type has its own strengths and

weaknesses. None provide a holistic response to LGBTQ people. Each one lacks in one area or another. And each one has failed.

TYPE A CHURCH

The type A church takes a stand against sin. Though the word *sin* isn't a popular term in today's society—and may even be dismissed as politically incorrect—we need to set this opinion aside and look at what sin is. At its most basic level, sin is any activity that falls short of God's expectations.

From this perspective, we realize that everyone sins (Romans 3:23). Everyone misses the mark and falls short of God's standard. Fortunately, through Jesus we receive mercy and grace for our sins. On a basic level, mercy is not getting the punishment we deserve, while grace is getting blessings we don't merit. Through Jesus, we can receive both God's mercy and his grace. This effectively deals with the problem of sin.

We don't need to change our behavior for God to accept us. He accepts us as we are when we believe in him and come to him in faith. It's a gift we can't earn and don't deserve. Yet he offers it to us for free.

It's in response to what he has done for us, however, that we later want to change our behavior. We want to sin less. It's a tangible way of saying thank you to him for what he's done for us.

Though God finds any sin distasteful, the church often groups sins according to their perceived severity. From this perspective, sins exist on a continuum from inconsequential to depraved.

For example, white lies emerge as a socially acceptable sin. Lying to avoid hurting someone's feelings somehow becomes justified. Overeating, that is gluttony, is often overlooked as well. We view murder, however, as a more serious offense, perhaps one of the worst.

Within this range fall various sexual sins. Though all are of equal gravity in God's sight, we look at them with varying degrees of acceptance or horror. These can include adultery and premarital sex, along with divorce and non-heterosexual activity.

Influenced by society's views, many in the church now treat divorce with nothing more than disappointment, even as inevitable. Similarly, sex before marriage too often becomes accepted in today's society, while adultery receives a more severe reaction. So, too, with the practices that fall outside a heterosexual perspective.

It's critical to remember, however, that this sliding scale of sin's severity isn't God's perspective but what his church made up.

Though the type A church correctly sees sin all around them, they ignore many shortcomings that they shouldn't and take a firm stance on those they find most distasteful. As such, they rarely mention white lies and often take a conciliatory attitude toward divorce, while speaking out vehemently against non-heterosexual behavior. And they often do this with vile vitriol.

In doing so, they not only condemn the sin, but they also condemn the person who does it.

Though they may feel justified in their opinions, this falls far short of the example Jesus set for us. His behavior was one of love, especially to the people on the fringes of that day's society. The only group of people Jesus criticized were the religious leaders—for their closed-mindedness, hypocrisy, and leading people away from God rather than toward him.

While Jesus offered love, these religious leaders offered judgment. This didn't please him. So, too, with the type A church.

An Extreme Outlier

There's one small church that has taken this type A model to an extreme. You've likely heard their name in conjunction with public protests against homosexuals. They use hate-filled rhetoric that offends most everyone and misrepresents the name of Jesus.

I'll not mention their name because they don't warrant coverage. And I'll not mention their message because I find it too abhorrent to type.

For an insignificant church on the far fringe of Christianity, they receive a disproportionate amount of coverage for their protests. I fear that many people outside the Christian faith—and those critical to it—perceive this one church's extreme reaction as representative of all who follow Jesus. This, of course, isn't true, yet each time this church receives news coverage, it reinforces the public perception that Christians are closed-minded, hate filled, and overflowing with judgment.

All type A churches need to be aware of this extreme from one small group of people and the damaging public relations that it produces. They must stay far from it.

JASMINE'S STORY

J asmine went to her first sleepover when she was twelve. It was with her BFF, Morgan. That night Morgan kissed her. Jasmine knew in her heart it was wrong, but it excited her. She kissed Morgan back. After that they shared secret kisses whenever they were alone.

Here's what Jasmine shared:

Morgan and I continued our friendship throughout middle school. We giggled about boys, but I didn't take what we said too seriously. I was more interested in her.

In high school, things changed. Morgan told me she liked Nolan. One day she kissed him.

That night she said that kissing me was disgusting and she wished she'd never let me talk her into it. I reminded her that she kissed me first. She denied it. She said I was lying and never wanted to talk to me again. Her rejection crushed me.

The next day she told everyone at school I was a lesbian and had tried to kiss her. That's when the bullying started. When they weren't pointing at me and whispering, the boys would ignore me, and the girls would sneer. Then the attacks shifted online.

It got too much for me. My parents decided it was best if I changed schools. At my new school, I used my middle name, Leigh. This would make it harder for the kids at my old school to find me.

I didn't allow myself to get close to any of the girls at school, and I didn't know how to talk to boys, not that I really wanted to. But I did date a few guys, even though I didn't like them or even want to be with them. It was a false front I put up to better hide who I really was.

Overall, I kept to myself and didn't share my struggles with anyone. By doing this, I graduated high school mostly unscathed.

I realized the truth about who I was in college. When I came home for Thanksgiving break during my sophomore year, I knew I needed to tell my parents and brother.

As we busied ourselves preparing the holiday feast, I summoned my courage, cleared my throat, and said, "I have something important to tell you."

A hush filled the kitchen and all activity stopped. They looked at me, but I wasn't sure what to say. At last I blurted out, "I like to date girls."

Mom smiled. "We know."

I don't know how they knew because I had just figured it out myself.

The three of them wrapped their arms around me for a ginormous hug.

"We all love you," Dad said. "Always have and always will."

Then my brother whispered in my ear, "I've got your back, Sis."

Thanksgiving dinner was late that year, but no one cared. It was one of our best family times ever.

But as Sunday neared, I had another decision

to make. "I'm not going to church with you on Sunday," I told the fam.

Mom's raised eyebrows asked a question, which I answered. "Pastor Tim says that homosexuality is an abomination, and we're all going to burn in hell."

"You know he's wrong, don't you?" Dad asked.

"I do," I said, "but I don't want to be around him or go to his closed-minded church."

In the end we went to that weird church down the road, the one with the rainbow on their sign.

It was a strange experience, and I'm not sure how much it was a Christian one. I felt uneasy the whole time, but at least no one there told me I was a sinner headed for hell.

Even so, I realized I didn't want to go to an LGBTQ church. It wasn't real.

Despite her unease, Jasmine's family attends that church each time she comes home from college. And for most weekends when she's away, they go to their old church, even though they disagree with the pastor's views. The whole situation eats at them.

They've talked about looking for a new church that matches their conservative worship preferences and will speak biblical truth but without judgment and condemnation. So far they haven't tried.

They doubt they'll find one anyway.

WHAT IS SIN?

*S*in is a politically incorrect word. Yet, as I've already mentioned, being biblically correct is much more important to me than being politically correct.

The politically correct society we live in decries the concept of sin as outdated, closed-minded, and condemning. The reality, however, is simply that these people don't want anyone telling them what to do. They desire the latitude to do whatever they want without repercussions or judgment. Yet when anyone does whatever they want, there are consequences.

We can best understand sin simply as falling short of God's expectations. Sometimes sin is doing things we're not supposed to do. These are sins of commission. Other times sin is not doing what we're supposed to do. These are sins of omission.

The word *sin* appears over four hundred times in the Bible, showing up in many books in both the Old and New Testaments. The Old Testament—where the word *sin* makes most of its appearances—reveals to us God's expectations for right behavior under the old covenant.

God's Old Testament standard for our behavior starts with the Ten Commandments, followed by 613 more instructions of what to do or not do as revealed in the law of Moses. Though some of these sins are easy for us to avoid today, others are challenging.

Everyone falls short. All of us have sinned. We all fail to meet God's exacting expectations (Romans 3:23).

James writes that if we stumble over one point in the law, we are a lawbreaker (James 2:10–11). If we lie, we break the law. If we gossip, we break the law. And if we steal, we break the law. If we cheat on our taxes, commit adultery, or murder, we break the law.

In one way or another, we've all broken God's law. We have all sinned. This is the reason God gave us his law. It shows we've missed his standard of right behavior (Romans 3:20 and Romans 7:7). It reveals that we can't earn our salvation by following a list of rules, of "dos and don'ts."

Jesus's Solution to the Problem of Sin

Fortunately, Jesus offers us a better way.

He fulfills these Old Testament laws (Matthew 5:17). He offers us a new covenant (2 Corinthians 3:6). In doing so, he replaces the first covenant found in the Old Testament (Hebrews 8:6–13).

The purpose of sin isn't to make us wallow in paralyzing guilt. This is a critical distinction. The purpose of sin is to point us to the need for a better way, for us to turn to Jesus to save us.

We see that Old Testament practices partially covered this through an annual animal sin offering to atone—that is, to redress—the people's sin. The animal died in their place for the wrong things they had done.

In the New Testament—the new covenant—Jesus becomes the ultimate sin sacrifice to deal with the issue of sin for the last time. It's a once-and-done, permanent solution to the problem of sin. To receive this forgiveness through Jesus—and be made right with Father God—all we need to do is repent of our sin and believe in Jesus (Mark 1:15) and then to follow him (John 10:27).

Our Response to Those Who Sin

Since any sin is enough to make us guilty of breaking God's Old Testament law, we may conclude that all sins are equal. And as far as our right standing with God is concerned, they are.

Yet it's our nature to categorize sins with varying degrees of severity. Whether we admit it or not, we treat some sins as minor or even inconsequential, with other sins as more significant or even unforgivable.

When we see these minor sins in others, we're quick to forgive or even overlook their shortcomings. Yet when someone commits what we view as a major sin, the tendency is to draw back in shock. We view the perpetrator as somehow inferior for having committed this sin. We're slow to offer them the same grace and mercy that God offers us. Even worse, we may never get to that point and ostracize them from our life.

We may judge them as having committed too great of a sin. As a result, we consider them unworthy of being our friends, refuse to spend time with them, or even opt to not be in their presence. We reject them because of their sin.

Thankfully, this is not how God reacts to us and our sins.

The better response—the biblical response—is to treat them as Jesus treats us and our sins. Like Jesus, we don't want to condone their sinful behavior, while at the same time, we don't want to reject them either. Instead, we should work to gently restore those who sin, while guarding ourselves from falling victim to the same temptation (Galatians 6:1).

TYPE B CHURCH

I n contrast to the type A church stands the type B church. Similarities exist, but they have many differences. The type B church also reads the Bible, but they're selective in how they apply it. They interpret Scripture through the current—albeit ever-changing—public opinion, embracing a flexible perspective.

They take the position that biblical passages which don't align with a progressive societal viewpoint are out of touch with today's world. Therefore, the text is no longer relevant. As a result, they feel justified—even wise—to dismiss that portion of the Bible as no longer applying. This is especially true in areas of sexuality.

Aligning with the current secular viewpoint,

they show themselves to be an enlightened congregation. Their website proclaims their openness, and their facility furnishings support their perspective. In addition to exemplifying Jesus's love, they strive to be inclusive, accepting, and tolerant. And they take a satisfied pride in doing so.

Their doors are rightly open to all, and they offer a warm welcome. The leadership takes care not to mention sin or the concept of sinful behavior. Their goal is to avoid causing offense or labeling any human behavior as wrong. They refuse to confront any actions that someone has thoughtfully determined to be what is right.

That's because they feel that confronting is judgmental, hurtful, and mean-spirited. They strive to avoid all three. For them it's a badge of honor.

The church is right to offer grace, but there is no place for mercy. Without the pronouncement of sin there is neither judgment nor the need for a merciful response.

People who receive salvation from Jesus in the type B church can do so with ease. Though they may later decide to change their behavior in response to what he has done for them, there is no expectation for them to do so. Nor is there any encouragement to try, because this church condones all sexual behaviors. This is the reality for their congregation.

Whereas the type A church is quick to condemn sin and reject the people who commit those sins, the type B church is quick to embrace all people, while dismissing their sexual behavior as irrelevant.

Each perspective has merit, but they also include flaws.

The type A church excels at proclaiming biblical truth, but they lack love in doing so. They fail at fully loving others as Jesus modeled.

The type B church excels at extending love, but they stop short of telling people God's truth. In doing so, they fail to speak the truth in love.

As a result, both types of churches need to reform their practices.

ROBERT'S STORY

Robert is a Christian and gay. He lists them in that order because he was a Christian first. Being gay came later. Because his church taught that homosexuality was a sin and had no place in the lives of people who profess a faith in Jesus, Robert kept the gay side of his life a secret from his church friends. Of course, his gay friends had nothing positive to say about church, so Robert kept Jesus a secret from them.

As a result, he ended up living a double life, with each side of his existence in constant conflict with the other. He compartmentalized who he was, pretending to be straight at church, while pretending to not be a Christian the rest of the time.

This is where we pick up his story:

Trying to live two lives, with each one a secret to the other, wore on me. I knew I couldn't go on much longer like this or I'd have a nervous break-down. My Christian self warred against my gay self.

For my own sanity, I had to let one side go. I held on to Jesus. That's what mattered more to me, for both this world and especially the next. I had to get rid of my gayness.

I prayed for God to purge me of my same-sex attraction. Over and over, I begged him for relief. Nothing happened. Though I dared not tell anyone in my church, lest they ostracize me, I sought help from other sources. I attended a healing conference. Nothing. Next was a seminar about receiving release from bondage. It didn't help.

I even went to counselors. But they didn't give me the help I asked for. They tried to get me to accept who I was and embrace it. But what I wanted was for them to fix me. Yes, I felt I was broken. I still do.

All this time, I continued to plead with God

to reform my attractions to men and restore me to his created order. I feel he's telling me no. Or he's ignoring me.

Not sure what to do, I pulled away from my gay friends and stop pursuing relationships with other guys. I still pretend I'm straight when I'm at church and around my Christian friends, all the while resisting their attempts at matchmaking.

I've pledged myself to a life of abstinence. Even so, I'm unhappy most of the time. And lonely. Why am I not attracted to women?

My only response is to strive to be in God's presence and place my identity in him.

This is indeed troublesome. Some people have asked God to move them from a homosexual lifestyle to a heterosexual one. And he answered their request. Others have successfully emerged from counseling with an attraction to the opposite sex. Then they met the right person, got married, and had a family.

But not all realize this outcome. They're left asking themselves—along with everyone else—why?

Perhaps we can find some solace in Paul's

struggle with his thorn in the flesh, an affliction from Satan (2 Corinthians 12:1–10). We don't know what vexed him so and can only speculate.

One possibility is that his thorn in the flesh was not seeing well. When Paul encountered God, he was blind for a time. Ananias prayed for Paul to receive his sight and he could see again (Acts 9:3–19). But there may have been residual side effects or long-term consequences. Some of Paul's letters conclude with text in his own hand, written in large letters. This suggests he had vision issues, but this is speculation.

Other people theorize that Paul struggled with same-sex attraction. As supporting evidence, they point out that he wasn't married. He also pledged to live a celibate life. Being unmarried and celibate doesn't imply a struggle with same sex attraction. Instead, celibacy is the highest form of sexual purity —for all people, regardless of their orientation.

Regardless of what Paul's thorn in the flesh was, it troubled him greatly, and he begged God to take it away. Three times he tried, and three times God didn't answer his request. Instead, God simply told him that his grace was enough, that his power shines through our weaknesses (2 Corinthians 12:9).

Though it might be trite—or infuriating—for us to quote this verse to everyone who struggles like Robert, Paul's experience does, however, provide potential insight.

SEXUAL IMMORALITY

As we mentioned, any sin is enough to disqualify us in God's eyes. From this perspective, all sin carries the same weight, since any shortfall we commit separates us from our Heavenly Father.

Yet from a practical standpoint, sins carry consequences, with some consequences being more significant than others. Such is the case with sexual immorality.

What Is Sexual Immorality?

To understand what sexual immorality refers to from a biblical context, we need only look at Scripture. Though we might assume this is an Old

Testament concept, warnings using the phrase *sexual immorality* occur mostly in the New Testament.

There's one lone verse in the Old Testament that mentions sexual immorality. You may suspect it refers to Sodom and Gomorrah, but it doesn't.

The one Old Testament occurrence of the phrase *sexual immorality* occurs when the men of Israel engage in sexual immorality with Moabite women. These pagan women use sex to entice the men to worship their gods instead of the true God. The Lord Almighty is not pleased (Numbers 25:1–3).

This doesn't mean the Old Testament is silent on the concept of sexual purity. The law of Moses lists—with squirm-producing detail—the relatives people can't have sexual relationships with (Leviticus 18:6–23). Personally, I'd have been much more comfortable with Moses simply saying to not have sex with relatives and leave it at that.

In the New Testament, Jesus warns against sexual immorality, Luke covers it in the book of Acts, and Paul writes about it to the various churches—especially the Corinthians. First Corinthians talks more about sexual immorality than any other book in the Bible. And John's epic end-time vision addresses sexual immorality, too, coming in at second place for the most references. John's revelation confirms that sexual immorality is something we must avoid.

Paul Looks at Sexual Immorality

Paul writes to the church in Corinth, urging them to flee from sexual immorality. He points this out to them because their church—as influenced by the greater culture around it—struggles with that sin. That's why much of his first letter to them deals with this subject, more so than any other book in the Bible. He explains that sexual sins are against a person's own body, whereas all other sins are outside the body (1 Corinthians 6:18).

Because of sex's deep emotional intimacy, sexual immorality profoundly affects our innermost being. It leaves deep scars, both physically and emotionally. That's why it's critical to avoid sexual immorality and control our bodies (1 Thessalonians 4:3–8).

Furthermore, we should have no hint of sexual immorality or any impurity. These are improper for us as holy people of God (Ephesians 5:3).

Paul and the other biblical writers throughout Scripture, however, never define sexual immorality.

That's because everyone knew what it was. But that's not necessarily the case today with our anything-goes attitude toward sexual behavior.

The dictionary defines *sexual immorality* as evil sexual acts that violate social conventions. Though societal conventions toward sexual immorality at one time had a mutually accepted understanding of what it meant, this is no longer the case. In fact, secular societal conventions have slipped to such an extreme that to many, nothing is sexually immoral anymore.

Moral Absolutes

Though society's view of sexual immorality has certainly changed within recent decades, the Bible's view of sexual immorality has not. Just as God does not change, his view of sexual immorality doesn't change either.

Most of the world claims there are no moral absolutes. Many assert that it's up to each person to determine what's morally right for them. This sounds nice. It's accommodating, but remember in Judges when everyone did what was right in their own eyes? Everyone did as they saw fit (Judges 17:6). This included their sexual practices.

In Judges, this attitude of each person choosing their own moral path separated them even further from God, and they fell victim to a series of oppressors as a result. Each time, they'd cry out to God for deliverance from a problem they created for themselves. And he'd repeatedly rescue them.

From the book of Judges, we learn we can't define what morality means at an individual level and expect our determination to please God and his exacting standards of right behavior. Since it won't work to decide for ourselves what is sexually permissible, let's embrace biblical teaching on sexual immorality as an immutable, moral absolute.

Beyond Sexual Immorality

Going beyond the phrase *sexual immorality*, Scripture prohibits adultery (sex between a married person and someone other than their spouse), mentioning it forty-five times.

The Bible decries prostitution (sex for money or personal gain), mentioning it thirty-six times, with *prostitute* showing up seventy-four more times.

Rape (forced or nonconsensual sex) appears nine times.

The evil of incest (sex between closely related

relatives) occurs once, but the concept shows up repeatedly.

Looking beyond the NIV, the KJV speaks against fornication (sex between unmarried people) thirty-five times.

We can, therefore, use these biblical passages to show us what it means to be sexually immoral. Lest there be any doubt, the meaning is never positive with any of these two hundred various mentions of sexual conduct.

It's clear from all these verses that sexual immorality is sex outside of marriage.

If our determination of sexuality doesn't align with what the Bible teaches, we're out of step with what the Word of God proclaims and what God desires for us.

Even if society applauds us for embracing their progressive views on sex, God does not. In the end, it's God's opinion that matters, not the world's.

Live Through the Spirit and Not the Flesh

When we yield to the temptation to engage in sexually immoral behavior, we're giving in to the desires of the flesh, that is, to our body and its physical urges.

Paul writes to the church in Rome to live through the Spirit and not through the flesh (Romans 8:5–12). People who live according to their flesh allow their minds to focus on worldly desires, on engaging in carnal activity. In doing so, they open themselves to letting their body govern what they do, which leads to death.

Instead, Paul teaches them—and us—to live according to the Spirit, God's Holy Spirit. When we do so, our mind focuses on what is godly and not what is worldly. Allowing the Spirit to govern our mind results in life and peace. Without the Spirit, we cannot please God.

If we live by the flesh, we will act in the flesh and die by the flesh. Yet if we live by the Spirit, we will overcome our body's desire to sin and truly live.

And to the churches in Galatia, Paul warns that whoever sows seeds to please their flesh will harvest destruction. Conversely, whoever sows seeds to please the Holy Spirit will harvest eternal life (Galatians 6:8).

We are to put to death all aspects of our earthly nature—our flesh. This includes sexual immorality, impurity, and lust (Colossians 3:5). To put them to death means to remove them from our lives, to cut them off.

In response to our salvation—our right standing with God through Jesus—we need to say no to all ungodly behavior and worldly passions. Instead, he calls us to live self-controlled, upright, and godly lives. After all, he has redeemed us from wickedness and purified us. We must hold on to this and teach these things to encourage others (Titus 2:11–12).

Conclusion

The Bible makes it clear what sexual behavior is acceptable and what is unacceptable. Paul, however, calls believers to pursue an even higher standard. Abstinence. Paul models this and recommends it as an ideal, but he doesn't command it. He makes sure we realize it's optional (1 Corinthians 7:1–7).

Contrary to the delusion of an anything-goes worldly mentality, as followers of Jesus we should adhere to the biblical teaching that sexual immorality is sex outside of marriage and something we should always avoid. And, if we can, complete abstinence is even better.

A PHARISEE, JESUS,
AND A SINFUL WOMAN

I n Luke 7:36–50, we read a story about
Simon. He's a Pharisee who invites Jesus over
for dinner.

Pharisees follow the law of Moses with great
zeal. To be sure they miss nothing, they adhere to
thousands more rules their ancestors developed over
the centuries to guide them in living the right way.
Few people today come close to matching their rigid
lifestyle and devotion. Though they're righteous,
they're also legalistic.

Jesus loves everyone, including the Pharisees
and other religious leaders, but we often see Jesus
criticizing them. Though they are religious insiders,
they miss God's intent to love and worship him.
Instead, they love and worship their rules for right

living. Jesus seeks to correct their perspective, but they oppose him.

With this as a background, it's unlikely a Pharisee would invite Jesus to eat with him. But Simon does.

The invitation, however, may be a half-hearted effort. When Jesus shows up, Simon doesn't offer him the socially appropriate welcome: to wash his feet, greet him with a kiss, or anoint his head.

Jesus, Simon, and the rest of his guests recline at Simon's table. Though we may envision them sitting on chairs around a raised table, they more likely lay on their sides, leaning on their elbows, with their heads toward a low table and their legs pointing out. Keep this image in mind as we consider what happens next.

A woman who had led a sinful life shows up. Though Luke doesn't specify the nature of her sin, leading a sexually immoral lifestyle is the most natural assumption.

It's unlikely the bigoted Pharisee invited her. This means she's crashing his party. With intent, she heads to Jesus.

She arrives ready to show how much she loves him—and, implicitly, how sorry she is for the wrong things she has done. This might be her only chance.

She stands behind his feet as he reclines at the table. Emotion overtakes her and she weeps. Her tears flow, falling on his feet. Without a towel to dry them, she uses her hair. She kisses his feet and pours her perfume over them. She empties the bottle. The aroma fills the room.

In his mind, Simon criticizes the woman for her inappropriate lifestyle and Jesus for allowing a sinful woman to touch him.

Jesus knows Simon's judgmental thoughts. The Teacher shares a story about forgiveness: Two men owe money to a lender. One owes a couple of months' pay and the other ten times as much. Neither can pay their loan and the lender forgives both men their debts.

"Which man," Jesus asks, "will be more appreciative?"

"The one with the bigger debt," Simon answers.

Jesus recounts how Simon neglected to wash and dry Jesus's feet, greet him with a kiss, and put oil on him. But this woman did all three.

Jesus tells the woman, "Your sins are forgiven." Then Jesus adds, "Because of your faith, you are saved."

The woman who was forgiven much, loved

much. This is not the case with the self-righteous Pharisee.

Though Simon held a critical attitude toward the sinful woman, Jesus modeled a contrasting perspective. He offered her love, withheld judgment, and proclaimed forgiveness.

Are we more like Simon or Jesus?

OLIVIA'S STORY

Olivia says she's both a lesbian and an Evangelical. She's been this way for most of her life. It's a challenging balance to maintain and presents a constant struggle for her.

Here's how she tells it:

Though it seems I've always been attracted to females, I won't say I was born this way.

In truth, I doubt anyone can honestly say that. Though it may feel like that for some people, it's more that those feelings go back to their earliest memories, so they think they were always that way.

Regardless, I won't say that about myself.

Some LGBTQ people get mad at me when I talk this way, but that's what I think.

Though I feel like I've been a Christian all my life, there was a time when I wasn't. I wasn't born a Christian, even though my parents were believers when I was born. I became a Christian early in my life, but being one is all I can remember.

The same is true about me being attracted to girls. It, too, is all I remember.

I grew up in a Christian home. We went to church each Sunday and on most Wednesday nights too. I loved the people in my church and treasured our friendships, both with the kids my age and with the adults.

Yet I also harbored a secret. I didn't tell anyone for the longest time—not even my parents.

I struggled with sinful thoughts but didn't act on them—for the most part. But sometimes I faltered. I felt shame for my lack of self-control. Guilt plagued me. I felt guilty for facing temptations too. I even felt guilty for feeling guilty.

My struggle was to embrace the truth that God had already forgiven me. I couldn't believe his love was unconditional. I certainly didn't deserve it. Nobody does, and that's the point. But it seems like a bigger stretch for him to love me considering what I struggle with.

As an adult, I did two things. Both were huge, and both were life-changing.

First, I took a pledge of celibacy. And by God's grace, he has helped me stay pure. I know I can't be gay and holy. My prayer is that I will live a holy, godly life (2 Peter 3:11).

Second, I told my small group at church my secret. They accepted me and didn't shun me. In time, I told more people at church. I suspect everyone there now knows my struggle and my resolve to not give in to it—with God's help, of course.

Out of respect for me, no one talks about it. Yet, if I bring it up, they listen and don't judge. And they pray for me when I ask. I also know some intercede for me even when I don't request it. It's a wonderful church and a great faith family.

Overall, I have a good life. I have a career, a loving family, and an understanding church. Yet I also wish for a special woman I could marry and share my life with. But that's contrary to God's ways and his expectations.

In truth, I'm often lonely. I know God should be enough, but sometimes I struggle to embrace that.

Yet, with God's help, I will persevere. I will finish strong and receive my heavenly reward. And that future hope sustains me.

Olivia's story reminds us to obey God and put him first in all things. This isn't always easy to do, especially when the world mocks our decision. But Jesus never promised us an easy life when we follow him. He does, however, promise us an eternal future, one that's beyond our comprehension in this world.

JESUS RESPONDS TO
SEXUAL IMMORALITY

J esus's detractors—the scribes and Pharisees —shove before him a woman caught in the act of adultery (John 8:1-11). But they aren't really interested in her sin. They want to test Jesus's reaction.

The woman cheated on her husband. She willingly gave herself to another. In doing so, she broke her marriage vows. The result is a blatant act of sexual immorality.

But what about the guy? If the religious leaders have genuine concern for the law they pretend to uphold, they should bring her adulterous partner along with her. It takes two to have an affair. But they don't care.

They have a double standard. They accuse the

woman of wrongdoing and let the man go, even though he is just as guilty.

She alone will face the consequences for their mutual act of indiscretion. The Pharisees bring the disgraced woman to stand before Jesus. It's as if it's a legal matter, with Jesus serving as judge.

They want to see if the Teacher will hold to the law of Moses in the strictest sense and sanction her execution, even though by this time in history they've likely veered from Moses's original command to stone adulterers. Or will Jesus deviate from what Moses taught and allow the woman to go free? Either way, they have a plan to use his response against him.

Let's imagine, for a moment, what this woman may be feeling. She was in the middle of the most intimate of situations—doing something in secret that she shouldn't be doing—when a group of men burst into the scene.

They pull apart the adulterous pair and drag her away. We may wonder if they even permit her to get dressed before hauling her off. She may be scantily covered or even naked. This only deepens her shame. Not only is her secret affair exposed for all the people to see, but so is her body.

She trembles. With her heart about to beat out

of her chest, her pulse races. Her palms sweat, her gut rumbles, and she's about to throw up. Besides her unimaginable embarrassment, she knows she could soon feel the pelt of rocks on her body, bringing about an agonizing death.

But these religious leaders don't care about the woman. They're exploiting her to trap Jesus into saying something they can use against him. With their vast knowledge of Scripture and their made-up rules about right living, they're sure they can twist whatever Jesus says to ruin him. The woman is their pawn.

But Jesus foils their plans. He doesn't take sides, something her accusers hadn't considered. Had he upheld the law or offered her mercy, they could have somehow twisted his words against him.

Instead, without pronouncing judgment, he says the person who is themself without sin may throw the first rock to kill her. No one qualifies. They're all guilty.

Jesus bends down and writes in the dirt with his finger. Though we don't know what he wrote, his focus on the ground diverts his attention from his detractors. They take this opportunity to slink away one by one, from the oldest—the most respected— to the youngest.

Having outwitted them, soon it is only Jesus and the woman.

"Where have they all gone?" Jesus asks. "Is there no one left to condemn you?"

"No one," the woman answers.

"Nor do I condemn you," the Savior says. "You are free to go. From now on end your sinful ways."

Too often, well-meaning religious leaders—and the congregations who follow their example—are quick to judge others for their sins when they should extend love and offer encouragement. This is especially true with sexual immorality.

Jesus doesn't condemn the woman, but he also doesn't condone her actions, her sin. May we follow his example.

Like Jesus, let us offer mercy instead of judgment. Let us offer love instead of condemnation. Then let us encourage people to change their behaviors without condemning them for their actions.

DIVORCE, ADULTERY, AND
SEXUAL IMMORALITY

A nother time, some Pharisees ask Jesus a question about divorce (Mark 10:1–12). "Is it lawful?"

Jesus doesn't answer them directly and instead responds with a question of his own. "What did Moses say?"

They know Scripture and have a ready answer. "Moses allowed a man to write a certificate of divorce and send his wife away" (Deuteronomy 24:1–4). Yet they misunderstand what Moses meant. The justification for divorce in this passage is if she is *indecent*. But we're left to interpret what *indecent* means.

If the woman was guilty of premarital sex or adultery, the law specifies death by stoning, which would make divorce a nonissue. So, indecent means something else, but it certainly doesn't cover whatever the husband deems it to be. Yet that's how the Pharisees interpret the passage.

Now Jesus addresses their question. He teaches about marriage and divorce. He shares God's perspective.

First, God created us as male and female. When he completed his creation by making man and woman, he proclaimed it as "very good." This contrasts to the prior days when he merely says it was "good." Adding man and woman, male and female, to his creation masterpiece made it become "very good" (Genesis 1:31).

In his perfect plan there are two genders and no more, regardless of how people today try to redefine it. We are biologically male or biologically female. By our created nature, we have a physical attraction to the opposite sex, which biology requires for us to perpetuate the species.

As husband and wife, the couple has children, fulfilling God's command to be fruitful (Genesis 1:28 and reaffirmed in Genesis 9:7). This was God's plan from the beginning of time. And since God doesn't change, it is still his plan today.

Regarding Moses's "certificate of divorce" provision, that was allowed because of the people's hard hearts, not because of God's intent. Instead, what God brings together—through their marital, sexual union—let no one separate. The idea of them being united as one flesh is a lifelong commitment.

To emphasize this, Jesus later tells his disciples that anyone who divorces and remarries commits adultery against his first wife. In God's eyes, both the man and his second wife are adulterers.

Yet in Matthew's account of this event, Jesus adds one exception. The only permissible reason for divorce is sexual immorality (Matthew 19:9). Various versions of the Bible use the words *fornication*, *unchastity*, *unfaithfulness*, *whoredom*, and "*some terrible sexual sin*," but *sexual immorality* is the most common phrase.

Therefore, except for cases of sexual immorality, a person should not divorce his or her spouse. And a divorced person should not remarry.

This is a high standard for marriage, one that too many of Jesus's followers have lost sight of in today's world. We must reclaim marriage as God intended and as Jesus taught. Divorce is permissible only in cases of sexual immorality and nothing else.

We must resist society's reinterpretation of marriage and misuse of divorce.

Marriage is between a man and a woman (1 Corinthians 7:1–5; also see Genesis 1:28 and Genesis 9:1 & 7).

When they marry, they become one flesh (Genesis 2:24 and Ephesians 5:31). Except for sexual immorality, divorce is not an option.

ADAM'S STORY

A dam's story is different.

My parents provided well for me physically and emotionally, but they were hands off in other areas. This included not giving me any moral or religious direction. They left that up to me to decide.

When I was in high school, a friend invited me to a sports camp at his church. I had a great time and soon started going to their youth group each week. It wasn't long before I attended church too. Soon I accepted Jesus as my savior. I was on fire for the Lord.

Though I loved the people at church and helped wherever I could, Wednesday night youth group was the best. I especially liked it when we broke into groups: guys and girls.

There's something magical about being with the guys and talking about faith. We had some deep discussions there. We connected. As a result, I grew closer to God and my faith deepened.

On the nights when it was just us guys, we'd end our time together praying. We'd sit in a circle and hold hands. At the "amen," we'd squeeze each other's fingers, let go, and open our eyes. It was a holy time.

One night, our prayer time was especially meaningful to me. With a final amen, I kept my eyes closed, basking in God's presence.

When I looked up, all the guys were staring at me. I couldn't figure out why until I realized I was still holding Blaine's hand. I glanced at him. His face turned red. He jumped up and ran out the door.

No one said a word. We all acted like it hadn't happened. Yet it did.

After the meeting, my youth pastor signaled for me to stay. He asked what had happened. I told him how I really enjoyed meeting with just the guys. And I admitted I might have a crush on Blaine.

He nodded and told me he appreciated my honesty. I assumed that was the end of it.

I later learned that the church council held an emergency meeting to deal with the "Adam situation."

Though they didn't kick me out of the church, that's effectively what happened. I wasn't welcome there anymore, not really.

Adam stopped going to church. He looks back at that time in his life as a phase and nothing more. He doesn't consider himself a Christian and no longer prays. If he had a faith—which he now doubts—he lost it.

Adam is now married. He and his husband have connected with the gay community. That's their place of belonging. That's where they find love and acceptance. Neither sees a need for God, church, or a faith family.

TYPE C CHURCH

A type C church is a stealth one. It may be a type A church in disguise, or it may be a type B church in disguise. No one knows for sure. It's a closely kept secret. Leadership is publicly silent when it comes to LGBTQ issues. They hope that by not taking a stand, they'll avoid dividing their congregation and all the drama that will follow.

People who attend type C churches assume the church's perspective on the LGBTQ issue aligns with their own, even though it's never explicitly stated. It may not even be implied. They adore their church leaders and relish their church family, so they presume everyone agrees with their LGBTQ views.

Though a type C church may have so far remained in an undefined middle ground, it's not a sustainable position. They can't maintain it forever. Eventually an event occurs, a question can't be side-stepped, or someone forces leadership to state their position.

That's when the illusion of congregational harmony falls apart. Though everyone assumed the church's stance would mirror their own, one group of attendees is suddenly disenfranchised.

It matters not which side the church comes down on, one group of people will be pleased and the other, irate. Sides will develop. Friends—sometimes even family—will find themselves in unwavering opposition to each other.

Their church's view does not align with their own. They didn't expect it and are surprised to not have realized it sooner. When this occurs, they're dismayed. They're mad. They stomp off. Many will find another church, while others will merely drop out of being part of an organized faith community.

The dissenting faction will leave their church home. In their wake will be a shell of what once was, struggling to continue as a sustainable congregation.

The same dynamic can—and has—occurred on the denominational level. A once-viable denomination hasn't taken a stand on this contentious debate. Member churches assume the denomination's view aligns with their own.

Then something happens that forces the denomination to proclaim their stance. Half their member churches applaud and the other half boo. Deep division occurs. There is seldom a way for them to continue to exist among their differences. Dissenting churches leave the denomination in the same way that members leave churches. The remaining congregations are discouraged, while the departing congregations are hurt and angry.

Type C churches and denominations—whether in truth type A or type B—exist on a precipice. Disaster will befall them. It's a matter of how soon it occurs and how bad the fallout is.

Being a type C church by not taking a stand will not last. It is not a sustainable position.

WILLIAM'S STORY

Two older neighborhood children molested William as a young child. This opened him to sexuality much too early in his life, way before he was able to understand it or comprehend what they did to him. The result was confusion.

It caused him to consider both same-sex and opposite-sex attraction as normal. He yielded to those urges with both boys and girls. This started his embrace of a bisexual lifestyle.

Here's what he shared:

I had an equal attraction to both men and women. It started at such an early age that I assumed it was normal, that it was who I was.

Being bisexual defined me, and there was nothing I could do about it. At least that's what the world told me.

Though my teachers supported my decision, my parents did not. But they still loved me despite how I behaved and who I dated. Despite the constant friction between us, I respected them for taking a stand—even though I thought they were wrong.

Their unwavering love for me prepared me to later accept and receive Jesus's unconditional love.

It happened as college wound down. I'd developed a reputation as a player, and no one wanted anything to do with me. I wasn't gay enough for the homosexual men or straight enough for the heterosexual women. That left me pursuing the few classmates who identified as Bi.

After a string of rejections, I was barely hanging on, not caring if I lived or died. That's when I became a Christian. Jesus made the difference in my life, but it was a gradual change that took years.

I realized that despite what my neighbors had done to me, being bisexual was a decision I could make. Paul wrote that we have no obligation to do what our sinful nature urges us to do (Romans 8:12, NLT). I so appreciate that verse.

Because of it, I embraced that truth and shut down that part of me. I stopped pursuing men, stopped flirting with them, and stopped going to where gay men hung out.

Instead, I spent as much time as I could at church. It was a safe place for me. There I met a wonderful Christian woman. We fell in love, got married, and began raising a family.

But I messed it up.

I cheated on her with a married man. Though God offered me mercy and forgiveness, my wife couldn't—not after it happened a second time.

We divorced, and I only see my kids every other weekend.

Let me be clear. I didn't cheat on her because I was bisexual. I was unfaithful because I was weak. My mistake was relying on my own resolve instead of depending on God.

As a heterosexual man pledges himself to one woman for the rest of his life, a bisexual man can do the same. It's just that a bisexual person faces twice the number of temptations.

We all face the temptation to sin in various

areas. For some this is overeating. For others it results in lying. Some people steal and others gossip. For me, the temptation is sexual, as I suspect it is for many people, both gay and straight. Though we don't give in to every impulse that confronts us, I gave in to my deepest struggle twice.

I fear the aftermath of my two moments of indiscretion will pain me for the rest of my life. Though God has forgiven me, I struggle to forgive myself.

Once I realized I needed to depend on God to deal with my sex life, my outlook changed. But it's a work in progress. My desires are still there, but less so. God is taking them away over time, little by little.

After all, you don't have to get clean before you get in the shower.

I've set my mind on heavenly things and not earthly (Philippians 3:19–20). I'm focused solely on my relationship with Jesus. He's all that matters. I'm not seeing anyone. I've pushed that aside.

Instead, with God's help, I'm being the best dad I can and praying for reconciliation with my wife.

Though many LGBTQ people say they're bisexual—reportedly up to one third—it's hard for others to see. If a bisexual person is in a same-sex relationship, people assume they're gay. If a bisexual person is in an opposite-sex relationship, people assume they're straight.

Regardless, our response to bisexual people should be love, grace, and mercy, just as Jesus gives us. Accept them for who they are, in the same way our Savior accepts us. Later, when it's appropriate —and not before—encourage them to change, just as the Holy Spirit does with us.

IF YOU'RE LGBTQ

I
f you identify as LGBTQ, know that the most important, universal, and unalterable truth is that God loves you. He loves you uncondi-tionally. He doesn't judge you for your lifestyle—even though some of his followers may. That's on them, and, in this respect, they don't represent him.

Jesus's arms are open wide to receive you—just as they are to everyone. He invites us to come to him (Matthew 11:28).

Unlike all other religions in the world, we don't need to do anything before we come to Jesus. As William said in the prior chapter, "You don't have to get clean before you get in the shower." Jesus accepts us as we are. We don't earn his salvation—

we can't. We need merely to receive what he freely offers to us.

Though we may opt to change things about ourselves after we follow him, it's not a requirement. Whether we stay the same as we've always been or change our lifestyle, we'll receive the gift of ever-lasting life and spend eternity with him.

As you follow Jesus as a LGBTQ Christian, there are four paths you may take. Though each follows a different route, they all end in the same place: in the new heaven and new earth that he will usher in at the end of time. There we'll spend the rest of eternity with him.

The four considerations are:

One: You continue to embrace your LGBTQ lifestyle. You decide to maintain that aspect of your life. It's who you are, and you won't change it. But you will strive to change other aspects of your life to become more like Christ.

Two: At some point you seek counseling to reorient your perspective. Though secular counselors will encourage you to embrace who you are, some will respect your desire to change. Seek a Christian counselor who uses biblical standards to shape their counseling practices. Though this doesn't guarantee success, it has worked for some.

To increase the chances for the outcome you desire, seek support from family and valued friends who will encourage you and pray for you. Prayer is critical, which leads to the next option.

Three: Jesus came to heal and to save (Luke 5:17–26). You've sought him to save you. Now seek him to heal you. Two thousand years ago, people readily embraced Jesus for his healing power but not so much his saving power. Today it's the opposite. Now people are more apt to embrace his saving power but often dismiss his healing power.

Seek a faith community who will help you receive healing of your LGBTQ leanings and restore you to a heterosexual perspective, one aligned with God's created order.

Receiving supernatural healing may happen immediately, but it could take time. Know that not all healing efforts today realize success, but some do. If you don't receive the healing you seek, know that the failure isn't Jesus's fault but more likely his followers and their own limitations.

When healing comes, it could be an immediate transition or a gradual transformation. Either way, surround yourself with like-minded followers of Jesus for support as you embrace the process.

Four: You may seek counseling and healing to change your LGBTQ perspective, but not realize the outcome you desire. Though this is most disheartening, don't give up trying.

Until you realize your desired results, embrace abstinence. Though living a celibate life when your body desires not to isn't easy, it is possible—especially with God's help.

But what should you do if you're in a same-sex marriage?

Paul gives some teaching we can apply to this situation in 1 Corinthians 7. In this passage, Paul addresses a convert with an unbelieving spouse. If the partner wishes to remain in the marriage, the believer must not divorce. The unbelieving spouse has been sanctified through the believer. The same applies to their children. But if the unbeliever wants to leave, so be it. They are no longer bound in marriage (1 Corinthians 7:12–16).

We can adapt Paul's teaching as a wise guideline for those wondering how to handle a same-sex marriage. Note that since God views marriage as between a man and a woman, staying in a same-sex marriage implies abstinence. This will be most challenging and may not be agreeable to your partner.

Conclusion: In all four of these situations, seek a supportive spiritual community. This may be a church, parachurch organization, or something else. If you can't find such a group, gather other like-minded believers and start your own informal faith community. You can't—and you shouldn't try to—navigate life alone.

LUCY'S STORY

Luke was born Lucy, a biological female. She enjoyed an idyllic childhood surrounded by a loving family and was encouraged by a supportive church. Her life was wonderful. Adults often praised her engaging personality, quick wit, and intelligence. But no one ever said she was pretty. At best she looked average.

Her appearance never bothered her, until junior high. That's when the guys took notice of other girls but not her. In fact, they ignored her. Though she tried to talk to them—relying on her personality, wit, and mind to get their attention—they weren't interested. That's when she knew she was not attractive like the other girls in her grade. That's when she realized she wasn't like everyone else and didn't fit in.

Here's how she tells it:

I didn't have the face and figure that the other girls had. They had what got the boys' attention. I didn't. Body image became my all-important fixation. Though I didn't need to be a girly girl or look like a model, I desperately wanted to fit in. Even looking average would have been good enough.

Try as I might, I could never get that cover-girl look of the other junior high girls. Though some of the guys had that model-perfect look, too, most didn't care about their appearance, and most girls were okay with it.

It was like a double standard. Girls needed to always look their absolute best, with perfect hair, perfect makeup, and perfect clothes. But guys could just be who they were and do fine.

I wondered what it would be like to be male, to not have to worry so much about my appearance. I'd be okay with that.

One day I put it to the test. I snuck out of the house dressed as much like a guy as I could. Taking the bus, I went to the mall and hung out.

I prayed no one from school or church would see me there. They didn't.

Assuming I was a guy, the kids at the mall treated me differently, even the high schoolers who worked there looked at me afresh. Guys my age would talk to me like I was one of them. The girls would smile and wave. I even got a couple of winks.

Exhilarated, I headed home wondering how I could experience this more often. For a couple of years it was nothing more than wondering, but high school gave me a lot of support for the idea. I considered it more seriously.

Over time, I changed my wardrobe, adopting the more casual, *whatever* attitude of the guys. Without my parents' knowledge, the school helped me move forward in my quest. In fact, they encouraged me.

In no time at all I was undergoing hormone therapy and moving toward surgery.

That's when I told my parents and the school to call me Luke and use male pronouns. The teachers supported my decision. Most of my classmates respected my request, with some even giving Luke more attention than they had to Lucy.

My parents didn't react so well. It emerged as a constant stress between us.

At church, however, I showed up as Lucy, all the while feeling like a poser. I was. But eventually they found out about Luke and didn't know how to treat me. I stopped going.

But it didn't matter. I soon headed off to college and completed my quest.

Lucy entered college as Luke and began with the surgeries to alter her appearance. Her parents struggled with this, wondering what they did wrong. Lucy's mom tried, but struggled, to call her Luke and refer to her as him. Her dad made no such effort. Though his lack of support frustrated her, she also admired him a bit for standing firm.

Lucy's story is like other teens and young adults who are unsatisfied with themselves and take dramatic steps to appear like someone of the opposite sex.

Some do it because of body image issues. Others do it because they feel like they're nobody. Being labeled as trans makes them special. And they crave to stand out in any way they can. Others have various motivations, but they all stem from a core dissatisfaction over who they are.

There's nothing wrong with wanting to better ourselves or change things we don't like. But we need to guard against extreme actions. This manifests in different ways for different people.

They don't like their friends, so they end those relationships and start new ones. Some are bored with their home, so they move. Others are dissatisfied with their paycheck, so they find a job that pays more. Perhaps the oldest of all frustrations is with their spouse. The new model looks attractive, so they have an affair. Divorce and remarriage follow.

In all these cases, these people strive to move from an unhappy state to a happier one. And for a while they may realize what they seek. But it seldom lasts. As they change homes, jobs, and spouses, the one thing they take with them is themselves. If they're not happy beforehand, they won't be happy afterward—at least not for the long term.

The same is true when people transition. They take themselves with them as they shift from male toward female or female toward male. If they don't like themselves before, they won't like themselves after. If they're unhappy before, they'll be unhappy after—perhaps even more.

In all these cases, people who make what they think is an essential change to improve their life realize the adage that the grass isn't greener on the other side of the fence. In fact, what they left behind may be greener than what they moved toward.

The truth is that God made us male and female in his image. No matter what someone does, the medications they take, or the surgeries they undergo, the DNA in every cell of their body never changes. At this base level, someone born biologically male will always be a biological male. Someone born biologically female will always be a biological female.

No amount of politically correct language or drastic progressive steps can ever change this reality.

PRACTICAL TIPS

Here are some practical ideas to consider in moving forward if you have someone in your life who identifies as LGBTQ. I share these as commonsense actions to guide your thoughts as you contemplate how to best respond. As you reflect on these suggestions, know that I am not a trained counselor or therapist, so treat these as steps to ponder.

May God bless you and direct you as you do.

For Everyone

Love: First, love them. Love is paramount (1 Corinthians 13:1–3).

God loves us unconditionally. So, too, we must love others. This includes everyone. There is nothing good anyone can do to cause God to love us any more. And there's nothing bad anyone can do to cause him to love us any less. This is unconditional love. We don't deserve it, but God offers it. And we benefit as a result.

Strive to offer everyone—regardless of their lifestyle—this same unconditional love. In the same way it would be wrong to love them any less because of their choices you disagree with, it would also be wrong to withhold love until they conform to your ideals for their life.

Though this is hard to put into practice, with God's help, we can move toward a godly love of everyone.

Forgiveness: Next, consider forgiveness. Jesus commands us to forgive others and we'll receive God's forgiveness. And if we don't forgive others, we won't receive forgiveness either (Matthew 6:14–15).

Is there anything you need to apologize and ask forgiveness for?

Before you say there's nothing, consider how you reacted when they told you about their decision or when you learned of their lifestyle. Did you say things you now regret?

Though perhaps your response was understandable, that doesn't make it right. Apologize, ask for forgiveness, and strive to correct your error.

Live at Peace: The Bible talks a lot about peace. Jesus gives us his peace (John 14:27).

Paul tells the Thessalonians to live in peace with each other (1 Thessalonians 5:13). He reminds the Colossians that as followers of Jesus they are called to peace (Colossians 3:15). To the church in Ephesus, he writes to be fitted with the gospel—that is, the good news—of peace (Ephesians 6:14–16). And to the Corinthians, Paul tells them God is a God of peace (1 Corinthians 14:33) and to live in peace (2 Corinthians 13:11).

Specifically, the book of Hebrews instructs us to make every effort to live in peace with everyone (Hebrews 12:14). Let's focus on this verse.

The key phrase in this verse is *live in peace*. This

should be our goal as followers of Jesus, to have a peaceful life.

We also see the imperative instruction to make every effort to do so. The passage doesn't say to make some effort. It doesn't say to make one attempt. And it doesn't say to try until it gets too hard. It says *every effort*. This means the pursuit of peace is an ongoing effort, one we must persist in until we reach it.

Next, the verse says we need to live in peace with everyone. This doesn't mean only our family. This doesn't mean only with our friends. And this doesn't mean only those we get along with.

Everyone means everyone.

This includes those who identify as LGBTQ. We must make every effort to live at peace with them. Anything less is contrary to God's command.

Seek Reconciliation: For those with whom peace seems impossible, we must start with reconciliation. Some relationships are so strained and so damaged that peace isn't possible until reconciliation first occurs. A preliminary step to living at peace is to first seek to restore our relationship. It matters not if the fracture is our fault, their fault, or both our faults. It's up to us to take the initiative to seek reconciliation.

As strange as it seems, Jesus elevates reconciliation above worshiping God (Matthew 5:24). This shows us how important reconciliation is to our Lord.

Paul says we have a ministry of reconciliation. This applies to everyone Jesus reconciled to the Father, which means each of us today (2 Corinthians 5:18–20).

And we see the ultimate example of reconciliation coming from Jesus when he dies for our sins to reconcile us—that is, to make us right—with Father God (Romans 5:10–11).

If God wants us to be reconciled with him, shouldn't we likewise seek to be reconciled with the rest of the people he created? This starts by showing them God's love and seeking their forgiveness for our wrong attitudes and actions.

Pronouns: What if they ask—or insist—that you use different pronouns, such as saying *they*? What about biological females who prefer *he* and *him* or biological males who prefer *she* and *her*?

One consideration is that by complying with

this request you show them respect. This eliminates a source of contention. Yet this also implies your support of their decision and their actions.

The other option is to continue using the pronoun aligned with their biological sex. On the positive side, this is a factual response, one aligned with truth and what you believe. On the negative side, it will provide an ongoing source of conflict.

If you do this, however, know that most of the world will oppose you for your response.

In a small way, I have some personal insight into this situation. My parents named me Peter at birth. And that's what everyone called me for the first several years of my life.

Yet kids delighted in teasing me about this name, snickering over what they perceived as a sexual connotation. Their torments vexed me. Seeking to avoid these uncomfortable exchanges, I began using the nickname *Pete*.

At my request, everyone began calling me by my nickname. From my perspective, it was an easy switch.

As an adult, however, I deemed *Pete* was not a

business-appropriate name. At least it didn't signify the serious persona I wanted to convey as a budding businessman. I switched back to Peter.

For most who knew me as Pete, this change was harder to make. Some made the switch, and others have not. My wife dismisses my repeated requests for her to call me Peter.

"I married Pete," she says, "and you'll always be Pete to me." She states this with an air of finality. Yet every time she refers to me by my nickname, I cringe. Compounding this, however, is that everyone who knows me through her also calls me Pete. And I also cringe a bit every time they do, all the while trying to offer them grace.

Initially, I'd say "I prefer Peter" the first time they called me Pete. But this was ineffective to get them to use my preferred name, so I gave up trying.

So when a person who identifies as LGBTQ asks people to refer to them by an alternate name or different pronoun, I can appreciate how they may cringe a bit each time someone doesn't comply with their request.

To be fair, however, no one can tell by looking at me if I am Peter or Pete. Yet many who identify as LGBTQ and request the use of a different name or pronoun may have an appearance that runs counter to the request.

In this way, it's easy for me to see both sides of this issue. I hope you can too.

For Parents

Parents feel sharp pain when their children don't follow their beliefs or sense of morals. In a way, it may seem like failure. As you agonize over this, you also hurt for your child's choices and actions.

You may ask yourself, "What did I do wrong?" or "What could I have done differently?" The most likely answer is nothing.

But even if you played a small part in your child's embrace of a lifestyle you don't support, it's critical to not focus on the past. Instead, embrace today, and anticipate the future. Don't dwell on what was, because you can't change it. Instead envision a positive way forward.

Love: As we've already covered, it's imperative to offer your child unconditional love, just as Jesus gives you. Show them—don't only tell them about it—your steadfast love. Though this may be hard to do from a human standpoint, it's possible with God's help. Seek him first and ask him to show you how to love them like Jesus.

If you want some specific pointers, consider the teaching Paul gave to the church in Corinth: Love is patient. Love is kind. Love does not dishonor. Love doesn't easily give in to anger. Love always protects, trusts, hopes, and perseveres. Love never fails. (1 Corinthians 13:4–8.)

This passage contains one more thing: love doesn't delight in evil. Instead, it rejoices in truth (1 Corinthians 13:6). Contemplate this. Then act accordingly.

May love be your guide.

Forgiveness: How did you react when your son or daughter told you about their decision? This may have surprised you or appalled you. Was your initial reaction disbelief? Might you have yelled? Did you say angry words? Call them names? Rebuke their sins?

These would all be understandable responses, but that doesn't justify them. Apologize to your child, ask for their forgiveness, and pledge to do better going forward.

After the initial shock of when you learned about the path their life was taking, what has been your ongoing reaction?

Have you pulled back? Have you withheld love? Been passive-aggressive in your interactions with them? Thrown Bible verses at them that condemn their behavior? Have you rejected them? Ostracized them? Banned them from your home?

Again, these are areas to apologize for, ask for their forgiveness, and move forward with the desire to do better.

If they have a partner, extend your thinking from beyond your child to include their mate. How have you treated them? Do they see God's love in you? Do they sense your love for them? (You do love them, right? After all, God loves them, so should you.)

Are they welcome in your home, or do they receive an icy reception? Have you made any effort to get to know them? Perhaps you've treated them so poorly that they avoid you.

You also need to apologize to them, ask for their forgiveness, and seek to start afresh.

A final item. When you ask for forgiveness from your child (and their partner), they may readily give it, but it's not likely. Don't expect a quick response or push for an answer.

More likely, it will take time for them to process your apology and request for forgiveness. It took time for you to be ready to apologize, so expect it'll take them time to respond. You may need to prove yourself to them before they believe you're sincere and are ready to offer you their forgiveness.

Also, if they've hurt you and you feel owed an apology, don't expect them to reciprocate. Though it may occur, it may not happen—not now nor ever. They may not even feel they've done anything wrong to apologize for. So the best solution is to let go of your hurt for how they treated you or didn't treat you. That's on them. If it is to happen, it will happen in their timing and not yours.

Pronouns: Your child may request you use different—and awkward—pronouns, such as saying *they* instead of the *he* or *she* you've used up until this point.

Alternately, your daughter may want you to say *he/him*, or your son may want you to say *she/her*. Along with this, your daughter may want you to call her your son. And your son may want you to call him your daughter.

Your child may also ask you to call them by a different name, one that implies the gender opposite of their biological sex or one that is gender neutral.

These are tricky requests, with no simple response.

As we've already covered, one option is to respect their request and comply. The benefit is it will eliminate one source of contention between you. The downside is it implies your support of their decision and their actions. If you choose this approach, consider if you will also communicate how you stand on the issue.

Alternately, you may persist in using the same pronouns, reference, and name you always have. This will provide an ongoing source of conflict between you and your child, but it will also clearly communicate your position on their request. Though they'll never admit it, they *may* respect you for staying true to your convictions and not giving in. If you pursue this response, make sure they know you love them despite your disagreement over what to call them.

Today's society excels at promoting gender confusion. But you don't need to be confused by the world's stance. And you must do whatever you can to ensure your children aren't confused either.

If you do this, however, brace for an onslaught from a progressive, politically correct society. They'll mock you as being closed-minded and say you're an unfit parent. They may even act against you.

As a thought-provoking illustration, consider Hans Christian Andersen's classic fairy tale, "The Emperor's New Clothes." In this story, two swindlers convince the king to wear a magnificent new garment that only learned people can see. The king and everyone else buy into the ruse until an innocent child asks an obvious question. "Why isn't the emperor wearing any clothes?"

Such is the case in the folly of using incorrect pronouns, where a child might ask the obvious question "Why is that girl pretending she's a boy?" or "Why is that boy pretending he's a girl?"

School: If you have school-age children, know that society is working against you. And they're doing it 24/7. Also, know that if your kids are in public school, your school system may work against you, too, attempting to subvert your parental authority.

You may need to take a drastic step.

Consider switching them to a private school, homeschooling your child, or moving into a supportive school district. All these are expensive options. I don't suggest them lightly. But your child's future is at stake. Do whatever you can to counter the anti-biblical programming their school bombards them with. This will give them the best chance for the future you desire for them.

If your child is in college, know that almost all post-high institutions work even harder to oppose your beliefs and to retrain your child to accept their progressive, secular viewpoints on sexuality. This perspective has even infiltrated once-respected Christian colleges. Ponder the options. Proceed only after diligent research.

Visits: If your child's an adult and wants to bring their partner for a visit to spend the night, this presents another dilemma. This is especially difficult to navigate if younger, impressionable siblings are present.

The struggle is balancing love with your moral standards. If you have space, provide separate sleeping areas and request they use them. Or offer to put them up in a hotel.

For Family

The recommendations for the families of LGBTQ people are like that of parents. The parental relationship, however, is unique. Though you may have grown up with an LGBTQ family member, you didn't give birth to them. You didn't raise them. And you don't have the same responsibilities that parents do. Therefore, different dynamics apply to family members. This also means that different opportunities present themselves.

As a family member, you have a vital role to play. God gives us our family. We can't change who they are. This is an unalterable fact, so we better accept them and embrace them—all of them.

Close family members could include a sibling, a cousin, an aunt, an uncle, a niece, or a nephew. Offer them love, ask for their forgiveness, and seek to live at peace with them, pursuing reconciliation if needed.

In doing so, you play a role that isn't available to parents. You may be able to make an inroad into a strained relationship that a parent can't. You may be in a unique position to take a critical first step that the person's parents can later follow.

Therefore, you may be the one person in your family who can restore a strained relationship with an LGBTQ family member. Don't miss this opportunity.

For Friends

Though we can't choose our family, we do choose our friends. Friends are a treasure that we must not squander. Don't throw away a once-valued friendship when it becomes hard to maintain.

Embrace the adage about the friend who sticks closer than a brother (Proverbs 18:24). Be that sort of person to others. Offer that deep commitment to your LGBTQ friend.

In addition to what we've already said about offering love, asking for forgiveness, and seeking peace, be there for them. Sometimes this means being present and nothing more. If they ask your opinion on their lifestyle, prayerfully speak the truth in love (Ephesians 4:15; also see Psalm 52:3).

Otherwise say nothing. Give them a safe space where they can be themselves. Offer them a sanctuary from life's storms, which assault them from every side. Be the type of friend to them that you want for yourself.

For Employers

Employers must take care to offer an equal employment opportunity (EEO) workplace. This is to avoid workplace discrimination. Additional laws specifically spell out the importance to not discriminate based on sex, sexual orientation, and gender identity or expression. (These same laws also prohibit discrimination based on religion.)

This applies in the United States. Other countries have different expectations. But since God embraces all people, shouldn't we follow his example in our business practices too?

With antidiscrimination laws, there is the letter of the law and the intent of the law. Ethical businesses should adhere to both. Many Bible verses support this notion (Romans 13:1–14, Titus 3:1, and 1 Peter 2:13–17, among others). Though there are some special-case exceptions, consider them to be rare and narrowly defined.

Businesses have a legal—and moral—responsibility to treat employees fairly and equally. This applies in hiring practices, compensation, disciplinary action, and promotion.

They also need to establish a safe working environment for their employees. This covers the obvious issue of physical safety, but it extends to other areas as well. These include removing hostilities that could detrimentally impact an employee's emotional and mental health.

An ethical extension of this applies to business customers too.

As covered in the section on advice for everyone, the previously mentioned practices of love, forgiveness, living at peace, reconciliation, and pronouns apply here as well.

For Coworkers

Employees also have a role to play in the treatment of coworkers—and customers—who identify as LGBTQ. The recommendations given for friends also fit in the workplace.

In general, show God's love to them.

Let Jesus's example guide you. May your actions and attitudes serve as a powerful witness to them, one that points them to Jesus.

For Churches

Churches can—dare I say, *should*—take the lead in appropriately responding to people who identify as LGBTQ. At the risk of repeating myself, offer them the unconditional love that God gives to everyone. They deserve it just as much.

Consider if you're a type A church, a type B church, or a type C church.

Determine what must change. Whether you're paid staff or a member of the laity, lead by example. Then encourage the rest of the congregation to do the same.

UNITY MATTERS MORE

When we talk about these three types of churches, it's easy for us to construct distinctions in our mind, to foster division in our spirit. We may align with one of these three forms—or at least identify with it more so than the others—while finding it easier to reject the other two.

The same reaction occurs—more easily and with less thought—when we consider the various labels that we sought to avoid in our discussion about these three types of churches. These entrenched and polarizing classifications include conservative, liberal, traditional, progressive, evangelical, charismatic, mainline, high church, low church, liturgical, non-liturgical, along with the plethora of Protestant denominations.

As followers of Jesus, we are wrong to let these divide us. There is but one church of Jesus, and he desires we get along, to exist in unity with each other.

This goes far beyond living in harmony with those who share our perspective about how to live out our faith. It includes all who align with Jesus. He is our commonality and the one essential aspect of our belief. Everything else is secondary. This includes everyone who is part of one of the above labels, as well as falling into one of the three types of churches.

We must live in unity with all who follow Jesus. If we can't do that, little else matters.

Unity means getting along despite our differences, despite our faith perspectives, practices, and beliefs. Unity, however, does not mean uniformity. If we were all the same, that would be boring. In a human sense, we'd have little to talk about.

Why should unity matter? Because unity is important to Jesus, it should be important to us.

Jesus's Sheep Pens

The apostle John records a teaching of Jesus about sheep, the sheep pen, and the shepherd—the Good Shepherd (John 10:1–18).

Jesus talks about a sheep pen with a gate. The shepherd goes into the sheep pen through the entrance. He calls his sheep, and they follow him into the pastures.

Only a thief would sneak into the pen another way. Yet the sheep don't know the robber's voice and won't follow him.

Jesus likens himself to the gate. In this way, he protects his sheep and keeps them safe. He won't let someone with ill intent enter the sheep pen. The thief comes to steal, kill, and destroy. But Jesus comes that they may live a full life. But he isn't talking about sheep at this point. He's talking about us.

Jesus, however, isn't only the gate. He's also the Good Shepherd. Although we know the phrase *Good Shepherd*, it only occurs three times in the Bible, all in this passage in the book of John. Jesus is the Good Shepherd. He cares for us, his sheep. He is protective, patient, brave, wise, and sacrificial. And he knows us by name.

As our shepherd, he cares for us, watches over us, and rescues us when we face difficulties. As our

Good Shepherd, Jesus is willing to die for his sheep. In fact, that's what he did. He died to make us right with Father God.

Yet sheep aren't too intelligent. They often find themselves in a predicament and need rescue. So too with us. As our Good Shepherd, Jesus cares for us, watches over us, and rescues us when we get into trouble.

When danger comes, the Good Shepherd won't run away as a hired man would. He'll stick around and protect his sheep.

Yet there's more. It's easy to overlook, but it's significant.

Jesus doesn't only have sheep in this one pen. He has other sheep too. They are in other pens. They also listen to his voice and follow him where he takes them. He'll get them and bring all his sheep together so there will be one flock, with one shepherd (John 10:16).

When we follow Jesus as our Good Shepherd, we must take care to get along with all the other sheep in his flock. This includes both those sheep from our own pen and Jesus's other sheep from all his other pens.

Through Jesus there is one flock and one shepherd. We are united in Christ. May we never lose sight of this. May we always strive to get along.

Jesus Prays for Us

As Jesus approaches the end of his time here on earth, he knows he's about to die. He'll accomplish what he set out to do and sacrifice himself for our sins to make us right with Father God.

Though he has many options on how to spend his last hours before he dies, he prays. It's his longest recorded prayer in the Bible and his most important one (John 17).

His prayer has three sections. First, he prays for his mission, its successful completion, and giving God glory. Next, he prays for his disciples, that they will persevere, and that Papa will protect them. Last, he wraps up by praying for his future followers—everyone who will one day believe in him. This third part of his prayer applies to us today (John 17:20–26).

In praying for us, Jesus asks that we will be one, in the same way he and his Father are one (John 17:22). Since they exist in perfect harmony with each other, he wants the same alignment from all who follow him.

Yet we have fallen short of this, far short.

As we meet with other believers, we associate with those like us. In doing so, we push aside those who hold an alternate perspective, even though we all follow Jesus.

As a result, we spend our time with people who think, believe, and act as we do. We elevate our own thoughts, beliefs, and actions as being best aligned with God. The logical extension is that we assume other viewpoints are wrong—or at least not as good.

This creates division.

But division is not what Jesus wants. He wants us to get along.

He prays for his followers' unity—*our* unity today—that we will be one. Our disunity works against Jesus's prayer for us to get along and act as one. Getting along is a great goal, but why is it so important that we, as Jesus's followers, live in harmony?

It's to maximize the effectiveness of our witness to a watching world. Our unity will best allow others to see Jesus in how we live our lives. This means our disunity weakens our witness.

If we can't get along with one another, why

would someone on the outside looking in have any motivation to join us?

Our world has plenty of discord. Shouldn't Jesus's church be a sanctuary from that? Instead, we disagree and fight as much as the world does, sometimes even more.

Our divisions, denominations, and doctrinal disputes send an irrefutable message to the world that the church of Jesus is a splintered, sparring group, unable to get along and unworthy of respect.

His prayer and his plan are to bring us together in complete unity (John 17:23). Don't miss this. Jesus wants us to be in *complete unity*.

May this unity extend in our response to those who identify as LGBTQ.

HANNAH, HECTOR, AND JENNIFER

Hannah came out in high school, and her classmates celebrated her for it. She moved through a string of relationships, with each one leaving her empty and lonely. Yet she hoped the next one would be *the* one. In college she pursued her quest with even more diligence.

Her latest girlfriend met her for coffee—and broke up, leaving little explanation. This is where Hannah picks up her story:

> I sat in the coffee shop in a stupor, trying to figure out what had just happened. *What had I done wrong?* I wondered. *Why do I have another failed relationship in my rearview mirror?*

I stared into my half-finished cup of mocha, no whip, extra chocolate.

Two women walked in. They were my age. I sized them up, but quickly dismissed them. They were both striking, but their reserved clothes turned me off. One carried a Bible. *Yuck.* I would never get involved with a closed-minded, bigoted, religious girl—no matter how cute she was.

The table next to me was the only open one in the whole joint. *Figures.* They flashed an apologetic smile at me and sat down.

Though they talked in hushed tones, it sounded like yelling to me. *Jesus. Faith. Prayer. Serving the Lord.*

I couldn't take any more of it. "Why don't you take your holier-than-thou-talk back to church where it belongs." I didn't mean for it to come out that way, but I didn't really care.

They both stared at me for a few seconds—as did everyone else around us. Then one smiled. "Don't knock it until you try it."

"What do you mean?" I hissed.

"Why don't you come to church and check it out before you judge us," the other one said. "Assuming you're not afraid to show up."

I'd show them. "Where and when?"

That Sunday morning, I stomped into church with something to prove. Not seeing either of the two women, I marched down the center aisle and plopped in the front row. I leaned back and folded my arms, daring someone to talk to me. No one did.

I don't remember any details about the service, yet everything that happened touched me deeply. It was as if it was all specifically for me. Something was happening inside. I didn't know what to think.

As the service wound down, something in my soul stirred. The pastor invited those who had questions to stay after.

I did.

Before I knew it, I gave my life to Jesus and committed to following him. In an instant, the Holy Spirit rushed into my body with a big swoosh. Tears of joy flowed. A peace I'd never experienced enveloped me.

At that moment, the Almighty removed the unhealthy sexual desires from my life and restored me to his created order. God delivered me from my sinful urges. He took away my attraction to women and replaced it with a God-given desire for men.

Hannah returned the next Sunday, and the one after that. Soon she became a regular and hungrily learned all she could about her newfound faith. In time, she fell in love with one of the guys at the church and they got married. They have two children with a third on their way.

Hannah tried to find fulfillment in her intimate relationships with other women. Yet true, lasting fulfillment came from following Jesus and experiencing spiritual intimacy with him.

Though Hannah's story is not unique to her, it's not universal either. Many long for God to instantly take away their same-sex attractions, but they don't share her experience of being immediately delivered.

Consider Hector:

I struggled for years to come to terms with what my parents taught me about God and the pull of my struggle over same-sex attraction. Eventually

I gave in and embraced the lifestyle that called me, even though I knew in my heart it was wrong.

During this time, I never walked away from God, but I certainly wasn't walking with him either. I kept him around as a safety net to bail me out when I was in a jam. But I barred him from the rest of my life, especially my gay relationships.

The devil deceived me that I could be happy and gay. Satan also told me I couldn't leave the gay lifestyle and was stuck.

But I had no peace.

I also sunk into substance abuse, although I didn't see it at the time. My work suffered, and my boss fired me. My boyfriend told me he didn't love me anymore and kicked me out of the house.

I was homeless, broke, and alone.

But God was waiting for me to come back. With open arms, he accepted me as the broken person I was. I recommitted my life to him and begged him to take away my same-sex attraction. Nothing happened.

I pleaded with him again and again. Nothing. I asked others to pray for me. Nothing. I went to healing conferences and deliverance seminars. Nothing.

I don't know why God didn't answer my prayers, but I know I'm much better off with him than without him.

It took four years of counseling to straighten out my thinking, but at last I'm free. I now see that God answered my prayer. But it didn't happen as quickly as I'd expected.

I'm now dating a woman for the first time in my life—and happier than ever.

God miraculously reoriented Hannah in an instant and he healed Hector over time through a godly counselor. But what about people who don't experience either of these outcomes?

Consider Jennifer:

It started young for me. I first realized my attraction for girls in kindergarten. Though I don't blame my parents for my gender confusion, I also recognize that had they not gotten a divorce, my life would have taken a much different path.

I kept my desires to myself for the longest of time and didn't act on them until high school. By the time college ended, I was in a committed relationship with the girl of my dreams. We were head over heels in love. I expected I'd spend the rest of my life with her.

We planned to get married. I knew she had bought me a ring and was waiting for the right time to make it official. I was happy, oh, so happy.

Yet at the same time, deep inside, I knew I was living a sinful life, that my actions disappointed God. Though I didn't know how I knew it, I also realized he loved me despite my lifestyle.

I later recognized that a seed of faith had been planted in me as a small child. As a young adult woman, that seed sprouted and blossomed. Jesus became more real to me than I could ever have imagined. I gave my life to him and committed to following him as his disciple.

Then he asked me to do something difficult, the hardest thing I've ever had to do in my life. He wanted me to break up with my girlfriend, the love of my life, my forever partner.

I didn't want to, but I knew I had to. I must. My faith and my future depended on it.

Afterward, I expected God would miraculously take away my same-sex attraction, and I would find a guy to marry and settle down with. That never happened. I'm still drawn to beautiful women and want to be with them.

Yet I realized my relationship with Jesus is what's most important. My identity is in Christ and not as a lesbian. He's not calling me to be straight but to love him.

Each day I pick up my cross and follow him. For me this means setting aside my gayness for his sake. Though it's not always easy, I'm pleased to do so.

Because of Jesus, I'm happy to be single and celibate.

We've heard the stories of when Hannah, Hector, and Jennifer sought God. Each experienced his grace in different ways.

We also talked about my friend David, and we shared the stories of Alexis, Jasmine, Robert, Olivia, Adam, William, and Lucy.

Each one is on a unique journey with Jesus. Some are just starting down that path, while others are much further along.

Regardless of where they are in their walks with

Jesus, they all need a community of like-minded followers of Jesus to travel with them. Yet where will they find this? Will it be at a church or some place else?

Sadly, today's church does a poor job at loving LGBTQ people in a God-honoring way.

TYPE D CHURCH

We've talked about three types of churches.

The type A church decries sexual immorality as a sin and proclaims judgment on offenders. They cite the Bible as the justification for their attitudes and actions.

In contrast, the type B church offers acceptance to all—especially those engaged in sexually immoral behaviors. They're quick to point out Jesus's example in the Bible as their justification for their open embrace of those involved in sexual immorality. They are right to do so, yet they fail to follow Jesus's example of encouraging a change in behavior, just as he did with a woman caught in the act of adultery. Though they're quick to say, "I love you," to those whose sexual practices don't align with biblical standards, they fail to add, "leave your life of sin."

And we have the type C church, which avoids making a public declaration on this contentious issue. Yet in doing so, they help no one. Eventually their true perspective comes out and some of their congregation leaves in disillusionment.

Finding Balance

In looking at what the Bible says on this issue, we see that all sin—including sexual sin, which is any sexual activity outside of a heterosexual marriage—is distasteful to God.

Yet we must balance this with Jesus's example of loving everyone, especially those on society's fringe. He forgives them, like he did to the sinful woman who anointed his feet. He doesn't condemn them, as he shows with the adulterous woman. Yet he balances this lack of condemnation—this absence of judgment—with a solemn instruction to stop sinning, to turn from a sinful lifestyle and head in the opposite direction.

Furthermore, we see Jesus affirming marriage as a lifelong commitment between a man and a woman. And, except in cases of sexual immorality, divorce is not an option and remarriage is adultery, for both parties.

As Jesus's followers, we should—we must—follow his example and adhere to his teaching in how we interact with others. But few people—and few churches—do this with any consistency or success. Yet this is the goal we should strive for.

The result is a fourth consideration.

A Fourth Option

A type D church warmly welcomes all. This includes those whose lifestyles don't align with biblical standards. Yet the type D church balances their open-armed acceptance of everyone with a willingness to speak the truth in love (Ephesians 4:15). This truth includes the fact that we have all sinned and fall short of God's expectations (Romans 3:23).

When we decide to follow Jesus, we turn from our sin and walk away from it. We leave it behind. It's critical to understand that leaving a sinful life-style—including a life of sexual immorality—is not a *requirement* to follow Jesus, but it's an intentional response of gratitude we have *after* we follow him.

In this way, the type D church best embraces a biblical foundation.

The type A church and the type B church both rightly practice *part* of what the Bible reveals, but it's not the holistic response that best honors God.

The type C church may fail to an even greater degree because they don't even talk about it. They fail to proclaim the biblical truth our society so desperately needs to hear or to even take a stand on this contentious issue because they don't want to offend anyone. In doing so, they risk standing for nothing and therefore fail to be a light to the world (Matthew 5:14).

An Informed Approach

The type D church should pursue an informed embrace of LGBTQ people.

In seeking to obtain an enlightened understanding, however, know that most of what the mainstream media and our politically correct society portrays is misleading. They are not resources we can depend on as reliable proclaimers of truth. They have an agenda, and they have their talking points.

Yet we must also take care to scrutinize the

validity of the counternarrative as well and not blindly follow every leader who criticizes the LGBTQ community.

Here is a place to start, which most people agree with. People who identify as LGBTQ are more apt to struggle with mental health issues than the general population. Suicide is a bigger concern. And their living situations are likewise sometimes less safe. They are also more prone to substance abuse. But don't take these generalizations as applying to every LGBTQ person you meet. For example, most don't have alcohol and drug abuse problems. But some do. Be aware that they may need help in these areas, but don't assume. Simply be ready to provide support if needed.

More importantly, people who identify as LGBTQ are more likely to be assaulted, face discrimination, and feel insecure in their surroundings. This should pain us deeply, just as I'm sure it pains Jesus.

The type D church (along with each of us as individuals) must strive to be sure to offer LGBTQ people a safe place to be—free of violence, discrimination, and threats. This bears repeating: offer them a safe place.

The goal of the type D church is to love everyone like Jesus.

We should also follow his example to call people to repent, that is to turn their life around. Just make sure this doesn't come across as a bait-and-switch strategy, where you first accept them as they are and later ask them to change. This is a delicate balance to maintain, but it must be pursued if the type D church hopes to accomplish their vision.

We should affirm that sex outside of a marriage between a man and woman is a sin. This isn't hate speech. This is biblical truth. Yet we must take care to speak this truth in love (Ephesians 4:15). When we proclaim truth without love, many will hear it as hateful.

Expect Opposition

The type D church, however, will face an onslaught of societal criticism for their pursuit of biblical truth as they embrace everyone because the world turns God's ways upside down. They proclaim that what is evil is good and what is good is evil. Isaiah declares woe to them (Isaiah 5:20–21).

Jesus says that when we follow him, the world will hate us because we do not belong to it. Instead, we belong to God (John 15:19). Another time, Jesus says we will be hated because of him (Matthew 10:22). And if we are not with him, we are against him (Matthew 12:30). To be with him means one hundred percent, not partially and not only in the ways we agree with him.

John later confirms that we shouldn't be surprised if the world hates us (1 John 3:13). And James adds that friendship with the world is animosity against God (James 4:4). We should expect persecution for wanting to live a godly life (2 Timothy 3:12).

We cannot serve two masters: God and the world (represented by money). Inevitably, we will love one and hate the other (Matthew 6:24 and Luke 16:13). By implication, churches and Christians that the world loves may not be fully following Jesus because, when he chooses us, he takes us out of the world.

Conclusion

God doesn't call us to be loved by the world, to be politically correct. In contrast, we are to be biblically correct. That's what matters most.

Though I'm sure type D churches exist, I'm not

aware of any—at least not yet. This biblically anchored vision for a type D church is what all churches should seek to become. In doing so, we will best represent Jesus to a world that needs him and grow the kingdom of God. And it starts with each of us pursuing this perspective individually.

May we—us as individuals and our churches as organizations—do just that. And with God's help we can.

As some brave pastors opened their churches to welcome hippies in the 60s and 70s, we must do the same today with LGBTQ people.

If you liked *The Christian Church's LGBTQ Failure*, please leave a review online. Your review will help others discover this book so they can read it too.

Thank you.

ABOUT PETER DEHAAN

Peter DeHaan, PhD, wants to change the world one word at a time. His books and blog posts discuss God, the Bible, and church, geared toward spiritual seekers and church dropouts. Many people feel church has let them down, and Peter seeks to encourage them as they search for a place to belong.

But he's not afraid to ask tough questions or make religious people squirm. He's not trying to be provocative. Instead, he seeks truth, even if it makes people uncomfortable. Writing from a biblical worldview, Peter urges Christians to push past the status quo and reexamine how they practice their faith in every part of their lives.

Peter earned his doctorate, awarded with high distinction, from Trinity College of the Bible and Theological Seminary. He lives with his wife in beautiful Southwest Michigan and wrangles cross-word puzzles in his spare time.

A lifelong student of Scripture, Peter wrote the

1,000-page website ABibleADay.com to encourage people to explore the Bible, the greatest book ever written. His popular blog addresses biblical Christianity to build a faith that matters.

Read his blog, receive his newsletter, and learn more at PeterDeHaan.com.

BOOKS BY PETER DEHAAN

Holiday Celebration Bible Study Series

The Advent of Jesus

The Passion of Jesus (Lent)

The Victory of Jesus (Easter)

The Ministry of Jesus

Thanksgiving with Jesus

New Year with Jesus

40-Day Bible Study Series

Dear Theophilus (the Gospel of Luke)

Acts Bible Study

Isaiah Bible Study

Minor Prophets Bible Study

Job Bible Study

Living Water (John)

Love Is Patient (1 and 2 Corinthians)

Revelation Bible Study

1, 2, & 3 John Bible Study

Hebrews Bible Study

James and Jude Bible Study

Matthew Bible Study

1 & 2 Peter Bible Study

Mark Bible Study

Romans Bible Study

Paul's Short Epistles Bible Study

Bible Character Sketches Series

Women of the Bible

The Friends and Foes of Jesus

Old Testament Sinners and Saints

More Old Testament Sinners and Saints

Heroes and Heavies of the Apocrypha

200 Old Testament Sinners and Saints

Visiting Churches Series

52 Churches

The 52 Churches Workbook

More Than 52 Churches

The More Than 52 Churches Workbook

Visiting Online Church

Other Books

Elephant God

Jesus's Broken Church

Martin Luther's 95 Theses (formerly *95 Tweets*)

Bridging the Sacred-Secular Divide (formerly *Woodpecker Wars*)

Beyond Psalm 150

For the latest list of all Peter's books, go to PeterDeHaan.com/nonfiction.

www.ingramcontent.com/pod-product-compliance
Lightning Source LLC
Chambersburg PA
CBHW082104140626
46553CB00018B/653